METEORITE

T0347784

Barbara Norden

METEORITE

OBERON BOOKS
LONDON

First published in 2003 by Oberon Books Ltd.
(incorporating Absolute Classics)
521 Caledonian Road, London N7 9RH
Tel: 020 7607 3637 / Fax: 020 7607 3629

e-mail: oberon.books@btinternet.com
www.oberonbooks.com

A catalogue record for this book is available from the British Library.

ISBN: 1 84002 401 1

Characters

HELEN
nine

ANDY
seven

LUKE
five

POSTMAN

COCKROACH

PREACHER

MOTHER

Meteorite was first performed at Hampstead Theatre, London on 4 December 2003, with the following cast:

HELEN, Lisa Jackson

ANDY, Michael Rochester

LUKE, Mitesh Soni

Director, Janette Smith

Designer, Rachel Blues

Lighting, Jason Taylor

Sound, Gregory Clarke

Deputy Stage Manager, Laura Routledge

Assistant Stage Manager, Sally Higson

The writer would like to thank: Anthony Clark and Jeanie O'Hare at Hampstead Theatre; Rose Cobbe, St John Donald and Giles Smart at PFD; Monika Bobinska and Emma Wolukau-Wanambwa for their help and support.

ACT ONE

Missing Letters

Scene 1

ANDY and LUKE's bedroom. LUKE's playing with his lego. HELEN and ANDY are discussing the PREACHER.

ANDY: (*To HELEN.*) I'm telling Dad what that man said.

HELEN: You can't.

LUKE: Tell what?

HELEN: (*To LUKE.*) Nothing.

ANDY: (*To LUKE.*) What that man said. About the meteorite.

LUKE is confused.

HELEN: (*To LUKE.*) Play lego. Go on. (*To ANDY.*) We can't tell Dad. He'll get worked up. (*Distracting LUKE.*) What are you making?

LUKE: Big shop with letters.

HELEN: Post office you mean.

ANDY kicks LUKE's post office.

LUKE: Dad! Andy smashed my post office.

HELEN: Sh! Dad's watching the news.

LUKE: He's always watching news.

ANDY: He made the potatoes all hard.

HELEN: It's the scratchy bits under his hair. It makes him irritable. He should go to the doctor and get some ointment.

LUKE starts to go out of the room.

LUKE: Dad! Andy smashed my post office.

HELEN: (*Trying to stop him going.*) Luke.You know when we went shopping?

LUKE: Presents!

HELEN: Your lego, that's right. Remember that man outside the shop?

LUKE: What man?

ANDY: He was massive. Big as a bus.

HELEN: He was wearing a silver suit.

ANDY: His face was shiny. Like a window.

HELEN: He was saying something. (*She moves her arm mechanically and mimics.*) 'A meteorite will come and blast your street to bits'. It's like the news.

LUKE is still confused.

A meteorite's this thing that comes out of the sky.

LUKE: (*Unsure.*) Mete-rite. Go away.

ANDY: You can't talk to a meteorite stupid.

LUKE: Mete-rite. Don't come here.

ANDY: Dad.

ANDY runs out of the room.

HELEN: Andy. Don't be a pest. (*To LUKE.*) Bedtime.

LUKE gets on the bed. A foil parcel falls out.

LUKE: Present!

HELEN: Gimme. It's for Mum. It's perfume.

LUKE: Can I give it?

HELEN: Not 'til she's home.

LUKE: She's been ages.

HELEN: Only a week.

LUKE: Has she gone to see Anna?

HELEN: Shush.

Pause.

LUKE: Why can't I have a letter from Mum?

HELEN: There aren't any.

LUKE: Did Mete-rite do it?

HELEN: There's a postal strike. Dad said.

LUKE: What's a post strike?

HELEN: It's when you get mucked about so you
    stay in your house and if you win they give you

lots of money. The postman did it. That's why there aren't any letters.

LUKE: (*Not getting it.*) Oh.

HELEN: Here. Have your blanket.

ANDY comes back wearing his bike helmet. He looks as if he is going to run out straight away

ANDY: I know what a meteorite is. It's a rock. Sometimes it's made of fire. It smashes out of the sky and *blasts* you to bits.

HELEN: (*To ANDY.*) What d'you tell Dad for?

ANDY: I only asked what it was. I'm going to blast it. I'll, get a rocket. With lots of water. Then I'll...

He mimes water flying everywhere. HELEN looks sceptical.

I'll get Marino's Dad's jetwasher. It's in his shed.

HELEN: He'll tell our Dad then they'll stop you.

ANDY is deflated. HELEN thinks.

Know what? That man, he said there's this thing, and if you've got it you can save yourself. (*Pause.*) Re, re-something. He said if you got some re-something the meteorite wouldn't bother you. I'm asking Dad.

HELEN goes.

ANDY: (*To LUKE, in a strange voice.*) There's this *rock* as big as the world and it's going to *blast* you. It won't blast me. I've got my helmet on.

LUKE hides under his blanket. ANDY jumps on top of LUKE.

Blanket doesn't stop a meteorite stupid.

They fight.

LUKE: (*Struggling.*) Helen. Andy's squashing me.

ANDY: The meteorite's going to squash our street.

HELEN comes back with sunglasses.

(*Letting go of LUKE.*) They're Mum's. You nicked them.

HELEN: I'm only borrowing them. Meteorites are very bright. The man's called a preacher by the way. Dad doesn't know about re-something. (*Sighs.*) I'll have to sort it out myself. (*Thinks.*) I know. Let's go outside and see it. Then I'll think what to do.

ANDY: I'm going outside.

LUKE: Yeah!

ANDY: (*To HELEN.*) Better leave him.

HELEN: He'll tell Dad. The preacher said it's coming at the eleventh hour. That means eleven o'clock probably.

ANDY: We'll be asleep.

HELEN: I'll set the mobile.

ANDY: I'll do it.

HELEN: 'Smine.

HELEN puts the phone by LUKE's bed.

It'll bleep at ten to eleven. (*To LUKE.*) I'll have to sleep here.

HELEN lies on LUKE's bed with the glasses on.

LUKE: (*Giggles.*) You've got your glasses on.

ANDY lies down wearing the helmet.

ANDY: I'm keeping my helmet on.

HELEN: I'm turning the light off now.

LUKE: (*Giggles.*) You can't go to bed in your clothes.

HELEN: Tonight's different, isn't it Andy?

Scene 2

There is a crackling, hissing and popping. A green light appears. It's coming from HELEN's mobile phone. It gets brighter and brighter.

HELEN wakes up. She picks up the mobile phone.

A distorted picture of the MOTHER appears in the screen.

(*Loud with excitement.*) It's Mum.

ANDY jumps up.

ANDY: (*Loud with excitement.*) Where?

HELEN: (*Loud.*) There's a message. Quick.

LUKE gets up.

LUKE: (*Loud with excitement.*) Mumma!

HELEN / ANDY: (*To LUKE.*) Sh.

HELEN: Look, it says 'Send your picture. M'. There's her picture.

ANDY: (*Looks.*) She doesn't look like that.

HELEN: It's a shadow stupid. Hold it. Hurry up.

HELEN gives the phone to ANDY. He holds it up to take her picture.

(*Calling.*) Mum, I'm sending my picture. (*Posing.*) I'm wearing your glasses. I'm only borrowing them. (*To ANDY.*) Press the OK button.

ANDY: (*Pressing.*) Okay.

There is a hissing, popping and crackling as HELEN tumbles through the phone.

HELEN'S VOICE: (*Distorted.*) Everything's gone upside down.

Pause.

LUKE: Is it Mete-rite?

ANDY: (*Scared.*) Don't talk rubbish.

HELEN appears in the street. Her hair is electric.

HELEN'S VOICE: Andy! I'm in this street. Come on.

LUKE is trying to see where the voice is coming from.

HELEN'S VOICE: It's easy. Just send your picture. There's this crackly noise. Then everything goes upside down. (*Pause.*) You're not scared are you?

ANDY gives LUKE the mobile to hold.

ANDY: (*To LUKE.*) Press it – there. (*To HELEN.*) Coming.

ANDY closes his eyes and holds his breath as LUKE takes the picture.

ANDY tumbles through the phone.

ANDY'S VOICE: (*Distorted.*) Everything's gone upside down.

ANDY appears in the street.

HELEN'S VOICE: (*Calling.*) Luke. Hold up the phone. Hold it backwards. Then press the OK button.

LUKE is pressing buttons randomly.

Luke?

LUKE: I want to see Mete-rite.

ANDY'S VOICE: Why have I got such a stupid brother?

Scene 3

The children are in a street. There is something familiar but not quite right about it. The houses and the sky have a sad green cast. There is a gatepost but it curves. And a wall which runs into the ground. And a tree with branches made of twisted forks and spoons. There is a sorting office but its roof is floating up. Empty sacks are strewn around.

HELEN: There's our post office!

ANDY: The roof's floating up!

HELEN: Look at all the empty sacks!

ANDY: The sky's all green!

HELEN: It's grey.

ANDY: You've got Mum's glasses on.

HELEN takes the glasses off.

HELEN: (*Uncertainly.*) I like the funny colours.

ANDY: Your hair looks weird.

HELEN: (*Checks her hair.*) It's hot.

ANDY: (*Checks under the helmet.*) My head's heated up.

HELEN: I'm dizzy.

HELEN leans against the gatepost but it's falling over.

The gate's tired probably.

ANDY: How did the phone send us here?

HELEN: (*Thinks.*) It thinks a picture is real.

ANDY: How will we get back?

HELEN: Through the phone... (*Realising.*)

HELEN / ANDY: (*In different directions.*) Luke!

HELEN: Come and see the funny street.

ANDY: Don't forget your blanket.

Silence.

What if Mum's not here?

A light appears in the post office.

There is a rattling, rustling and fluttering.

A wind is blowing.

There's someone there. (*Uncertain.*) Mum?

ANDY tightens his helmet.

HELEN puts the glasses back on.

The POSTMAN appears. He's wearing glasses. He's very small and very thin. His hair is long and straggly. He walks against the wind with a shuffle and a stoop. He carries a sad, empty red bag, faded in the green light.

It's the postman.

HELEN: Let's ask him if he's got our letters.

HELEN / ANDY: Scuse me. Have you got any letters?

HELEN: We haven't had any.

ANDY: For ages.

The wind is very strong.

POSTMAN: You're a funny couple of kids.

ANDY: We're not a couple. We've got a brother. His name's Luke. He couldn't make it.

HELEN: And we had a baby sister. Her name was Anna. She was really little but she died.

The POSTMAN wipes away a tear.

ANDY: It was ages ago.

HELEN: Before the holidays. Things like that happen sometimes.

POSTMAN: Your Mum took it hard I expect.

ANDY: She's okay. She doesn't cry. Sometimes her face goes funny.

HELEN: And her eyes go red but that's because she's tired.

ANDY: Have you seen her?

The POSTMAN shakes his head.

HELEN: (*Pause.*) She's away at the moment. She's definitely sent some letters.

They glance at his bag.

POSTMAN: I hope you get some good news soon.

He walks off, struggling against the wind.

HELEN: (*After the POSTMAN.*) We know there was this postal strike.

The POSTMAN stops. He seems upset.

You could sit down and tell us all about it.

She leads the POSTMAN to the gatepost.

He sits down. He takes out a piece of silver foil.

The children stare.

The POSTMAN puts the foil on his head as a kind of hat.

The sky brightens.

ANDY: (*To HELEN.*) I'm looking in his bag. (*To POSTMAN.*) I'll just hang it up.

ANDY hangs the POSTMAN's bag on the gatepost. It's obviously empty. He checks inside.

Where've all your letters gone?

HELEN: Did you lose the strike?

POSTMAN: (*Sighs.*) There wasn't any strike. I've done my round, every day. I was walking along with my bag full of letters. Suddenly the sky turned green. Then this wind began to blow. There was a rustling and a fluttering in my mailbag and all the letters flew into the sky.

Pause.

ANDY: He's talking rubbish probably.

HELEN: (*To ANDY.*) Sh.

POSTMAN: My wife says that. She says I'm a useless postman. If I don't find the letters I'm going to get the sack.

He looks as if he's going to cry.

HELEN: (*Quickly.*) We don't think you're useless.

An extra strong gust of wind blows.

ANDY: Why's it so windy?

POSTMAN: (*Cheering up at the interest.*) We're passing through a rocky patch of space. Meteorites all around. Get one a long way off, you have rattling and rustling and the sky turns green. Get a big one landing, you have the roads dug up and the houses on fire. I read it in a magazine. I get a lot of magazines in my bag.

ANDY: You're not supposed to read them. You're supposed to take them to the right houses.

HELEN: (*Quickly.*) We know about the meteorite. (*Looks at the sky.*) It must still be a long way off.

POSTMAN: (*Confidentially.*) Sometimes I hear a crackling, a hissing and a popping... Terrible racket.

HELEN: (*Excited.*) I heard a noise like that when I came through the... (*Stops herself.*)

POSTMAN: (*To HELEN. Excited.*) It's those glasses of yours. And the long hair. They pick up (*Confidentially.*) Very Low Frequencies. It's not everyone can hear meteorites.

ANDY: (*To everyone. Frustrated.*) Don't talk rubbish.

POSTMAN: (*Upset at this but trying to ignore it.*) They don't like silver foil, that's what I read. Always carry some with me. Pop a bit of foil on your head and you won't have any trouble from meteorites.

HELEN: (*To POSTMAN.*) We know how to stop it thank you. (*To ANDY.*) I think he's a bit weird.

ANDY: (*To HELEN.*) He's a useless postman. He just lost our letters probably. (*To POSTMAN.*) You should get the sack.

The POSTMAN cries uncontrollably.

He dissolves into a puddle of tears.

HELEN: (*To ANDY.*) Now look what you've done. (*After POSTMAN.*) You can stay and help us if you like. He's turned into a puddle.

Scene 4

The street. The sky is still green.

HELEN: The wind's stopped. It must be nearly the eleventh hour. I'll just check... (*Realising the phone's missing.*) Oh no. Luke. We need the mobile now.

Pause.

ANDY: What's that?

A letter floats down.

HELEN: It's a letter.

Two more float down.

HELEN and ANDY try to catch them so they don't fall in the puddle.

ANDY: They'll get wet.

HELEN tries to read an address.

HELEN: The writing's all wobbly.

ANDY tries to read one.

ANDY: This one's smudged.

HELEN: (*Startled.*) This one says Anna. Let's open it. (*Pause.*) We can't. It says Private.

The sky goes dark.

ANDY: Oh no.

LUKE'S VOICE: (*Distorted.*) Everything's gone upside down.

When the sky lightens, it is green again.

LUKE is there, holding the mobile phone.

He's dragging the blanket after him.

LUKE: I pressed all the buttons.

ANDY: Why did you bring your blanket stupid?

HELEN: (*Pleased.*) Luke. We've got some letters. There wasn't a post strike. The wind blew them up into the sky. This one's for you.

HELEN gives a letter to LUKE.

LUKE: (*Excited.*) Mumma!

ANDY pushes LUKE over. He grabs the mobile.

ANDY: Gimme.

LUKE: My head's hot. Why's the sky all green?

HELEN: (*To LUKE.*) The meteorite's coming but it's a long way off thank goodness. Open the letter. Hurry up.

LUKE opens his letter.

A hat falls out.

He gives the letter to HELEN to read.

LUKE: (*Excited.*) What does it say?

ANDY: It's a bill probably.

HELEN: It says: (*Reads.*) You can wear this hat when you feel sad.

ANDY: (*Pleased.*) See. It's rubbish.

HELEN: The rest's smudged. (*To LUKE.*) Put the hat on.

LUKE puts the hat on.

He laughs.

The sky brightens.

LUKE: I've got a hat from Mumma.

ANDY: I've got my helmet. (*He knocks on it.*)

HELEN opens another letter.

HELEN: Maybe I've got a hat.

There's a very small square in it.

(*Disappointed.*) It's really small.

She starts to unfold it.

It isn't a hat.

She unfolds it some more.

It's a map or something.

ANDY picks up another letter.

ANDY: This one's for me.

He opens it.

(*Reads.*) Get Dad to make you potato croakits. (*Excited.*) Yeah. It's definitely from Mum. (*Reads.*) Don't...

Pause.

HELEN: What?

ANDY tries to hide the letter.

ANDY: It's smudged.

HELEN grabs it and reads.

HELEN: (*Reading.*) Don't throw any more stones through Marino's Dad's window. Ha ha.

ANDY doesn't laugh. He checks inside the envelope.

ANDY: It's a hat. I don't want it. (*He stuffs the hat in his pocket.*) I'm opening this one.

ANDY opens ANNA's letter.

HELEN: You can't.

ANDY: There's nothing in it. Just some hair.

HELEN: It's a curl. (*Pause.*) Better put it back.

ANDY does. HELEN starts to unfold the map.

It's massive. Give us a hand

LUKE is looking at the tree.

ANDY is sulking.

ANDY: Why's she so cross? Didn't throw stones.

HELEN: (*Hardly listening.*) Okay. You didn't. There's an arrow going round. Ready?

ANDY takes one side of the map. They spin round.

ANDY: I'm dizzy.

HELEN: Stop!

They stop. HELEN peers at it. She puts the glasses on.

It says: 'The Garden of Re-pentance'.

LUKE has climbed up to reach a branch.

ANDY: Luke. What are you doing?

The tree is laden with potato croquettes. LUKE picks one.

LUKE: Potato crockits!

HELEN: Croquettes, not crockits. Come down. We've got to look at the map.

LUKE: It's hot!

LUKE starts to eat the potato croquette.

ANDY climbs up.

ANDY: The branches are all twisted. They're made of forks and spoons! Potato croakits!

ANDY shoves LUKE out of the way. He eats a croquette.

HELEN: We could have one or two.

HELEN drops the map. She climbs the tree. She picks and eats a potato croquette.

Music. Together and as fast as they can, the children pick as many potato croquettes as possible and make a big pile on the outspread map which HELEN seems to have forgotten about.

LUKE uses his blanket to transport his croquettes which gives him an advantage in carrying but less time to eat.

ANDY tries to prevent LUKE eating any potato croquettes at all but when this fails and he has eaten enough himself he begins to pelt LUKE with them.

HELEN eats more than anyone, but surreptitiously.

The music stops.

LUKE: I'm full up.

HELEN: I'm bursting.

HELEN and LUKE yawn, making contented tunes.

LUKE: Sleepy.

LUKE gets under his blanket.

HELEN: I'll just sleep for a little while.

They yawn again. HELEN lies down on the map.

(*Sleepily.*) I'll check the time in a minute. It must be nearly the eleventh...

HELEN is asleep.

ANDY: (*Cross.*) I suppose you're all going to sleep now.

ANDY lies down to sleep.

END OF ACT ONE.

ACT TWO

The Garden of Repentance

Scene 1

The children are sleeping, LUKE and HELEN on the outspread map. The shadow of a strange bird shaped like a letter passes over. It sings a sad tune.

LUKE wakes up. His hat falls off.

The sky turns green.

LUKE: Helen! Andy!

LUKE knocks on ANDY's helmet.

Wake. Up.

ANDY: (*Without moving.*) Tummy ache.

ANDY goes back to sleep.

HELEN wakes up.

LUKE: Andy's got a tummy ache. He ate twenty-seven potato crockits.

HELEN: Ugh.

She jumps up. She sees the map is creased and dirty.

Oh no. The map. (*Tries to read.*) There's crumbs everywhere. Let's shake it.

They shake out the map.

HELEN tries to read it. She puts the glasses on, panicking.

Now it's too grey.

She takes them off.

Now it's too green. I wish the sky would cheer up.

LUKE: Mete-rite. We're sick of green. Can you wear something else please?

Pause. They sigh.

HELEN: Put your hat on a minute.

LUKE does. The green light goes.

See that.

LUKE: What?

HELEN: Take it off.

He does. The green light returns.

(*Quickly.*) Put it on.

LUKE puts his hat on. The green light goes.

LUKE: (*Laughs.*) Mete-rite doesn't like my hat.

HELEN: It makes the sky cheerful.

HELEN can now see the map.

That's better. (*Reads.*) The Garden of Re-pentance.

LUKE: What's Garden of Re-Petals?

HELEN: It's, a garden. Mum wants us to get some Re-pentance probably.

HELEN starts walking.

Hurry up.

LUKE: Can blankit come?

HELEN: Leave it with Andy. (*Reading the map.*) It's miles...

LUKE looks as if he's not going to come.

LUKE: Can Andy come?

HELEN: He's being a pest. Mum said in her letter. Better let him sleep it off. You can stay here if you want.

LUKE takes his blanket.

HELEN is contorting herself to read the map.

HELEN: The arrow goes round (*Reading.*) 'The Tree of Delight'. Then it goes over 'The Gatepost of Despair'. Then it goes down 'The Irritability Steps'. Everything's got funny names.

They walk round the tree, climb over the gatepost and go.

Scene 2

The sky is pink tinged.

There is a gate beyond which is a rose garden.

A sign reads 'The Garden of Repentance'. Beneath that there is a notice which reads:

PRIVATE PROPERTY: NO RIGHT OF WAY. NO BALL GAMES. NO FLOWER PICKING.

Beside the gate is a large pile of rubbish.

HELEN and LUKE enter.

HELEN is reading the map.

HELEN: Cross the Tragedy Underpass by the footbridge. Done that. Join the Gyratory System of Unreality. Someone should think of sensible names. Go round the Sleepless Nights Roundabout three times and take the second exit. On the Dual Carriageway of Crying and Sighing stick to the Hard Shoulder until you reach the Relief Road. You will come to the Level Crossing of Lack of Initiative. (*Annoyed as she loses her place on the map. They stop.*) Let's go back. (*Finding her place again.*) Step over Your-Fault Line. At Jittery Junction, take the right fork. Follow the track marked Wandering Aimlessly...

LUKE: (*Smells.*) It smells lovely. Like Mum's perfume.

HELEN looks up from the map.

HELEN: (*Reads.*) 'The Garden of Re-pentance. Private Property. No Right of Way. No ball games. No flower picking.' (*Sees rubbish.*) Ugh. Look at that rubbish. Mum says people should know better.

HELEN looks through the bars of the gate into the garden.

There's rows and rows of roses. (*Shocked.*) It says Anna. It's written in the flowers.

LUKE: (*Excited.*) Will Mum be inside?

HELEN: I can't see any re-pent...

There is a loud creak.

HELEN and LUKE freeze.

The pile of rubbish begins to move.

Two antennae appear. They wave angrily at the children.

HELEN: (*To LUKE.*) Stay still.

The rubbish moves again.

The antennae push further out. At their base is a hard head like ANDY's helmet.

More creaking.

LUKE: Is it Mete-rite?

HELEN: I think it's a sort of pest.

LUKE: Is it Andy?

HELEN and LUKE run and hide behind the gatepost.

The cockroach creaks loudly.

Its antennae wave wildly.

HELEN: Let's pretend to be another pest.

LUKE: Blankit will hide us.

HELEN: (*She sighs, then realising there's no better idea.*) Hold onto me. You have to creak very loud. When I kick you, crawl behind me under blanket. I'll do the talking.
Got it?

LUKE: Okay.

Music as HELEN and LUKE form an improbable insect under the blanket, LUKE creaking, HELEN waving one arm in front.

They set off towards the gate.

They are about to reach the gate but before HELEN can give the signal, the COCKROACH speaks.

Music stops.

COCKROACH: Nice morning. Won't last.

HELEN and LUKE stop.

HELEN: (*Worried.*) Is it morning already?

COCKROACH: Red sky. (*Sighs.*) It's a warning.

HELEN: (*To COCKROACH.*) Is this the Garden of Re-pentance?

COCKROACH: Can't you smell?

HELEN: (*Annoyed.*) Of course I can. So is there any Re-pentance in the garden?

The COCKROACH laughs, his antennae waving wildly.

COCKROACH: City cockroach are you?

HELEN: (COCKROACH.) I'm not a cockroach.

The COCKROACH laughs wildly.

COCKROACH: Could have fooled me.

HELEN: (*Quickly.*) I am a cockroach really. Sometimes I forget.

COCKROACH: It's the smell.

HELEN: (*Annoyed.*) I don't smell.

COCKROACH: (*Wearily.*) The garden's full of roses. But Repentance isn't the roses as such. It's the smell of roses.

HELEN: I'd like to smell some please.

COCKROACH: Don't tell me. You haven't got a Visitor's Pass. (*Confidentially.*) There's someone in there already. A pest. Human. Female.

HELEN: (*Excited.*) Who?

COCKROACH: (*Confidentially.*) Couldn't stop her. Seemed to be in a right old tizzy. Lost her baby while she was asleep. Blames herself. (*Snorts.*) Pests take these things to heart. Guess how many brothers and sisters I had? Five thousand six hundred and sixty-six.

HELEN: (*Politely.*) That's a lot.

COCKROACH: All of them kicked the bucket. Pests use sprays, that's the problem. (*Indignant.*) This pest, she looked down her nose at my rubbish. (*Snorts.*) Who makes the rubbish in the first place? Cockroaches or pests?

The COCKROACH laughs wildly and kicks some rubbish around.

HELEN: (*Impatient.*) The thing is I need some Repentance. It's an emergency.

COCKROACH: Meteorite is it?

HELEN: Sorry?

COCKROACH: Repentance saves you from meteorites.

HELEN is startled.

Boss says so anyway. (*Confidentially.*) He cuts the heads off the roses, then he strips the petals, then he stamps on them. I help him with that, lot of feet. Looking for a job?

HELEN shakes her head. The glasses fall off. She doesn't notice.

Then he squeezes the juice into bottles. Flogs them down the West End. That's Repentance. Doesn't come cheap.

HELEN: So if the garden's full of Repentance, the meteorite can't get in?

The COCKROACH looks at her strangely.

COCKROACH: Meteorites don't bother me. It's Repentance I don't like. Ugh. Gives me terrible hayfever.

He wipes away a tear.

Boss says I'm putting it on. One of these days he'll be sorry. I'll drown in my own tears

LUKE is getting impatient.

Go on. Have a good sniff if that's your poison. In you go. I won't tell the Boss if you're quick.

HELEN kicks LUKE under the blanket.

They drop to the ground and, keeping the blanket over them, wriggle under the gate.

Scene 3

The children are inside the Garden of Repentance.

The sky is a fierier pink.

There are rows and rows of roses.

There's no sign of the MOTHER or ANNA.

HELEN: (*Searching.*) It was there before. It said Anna in the roses. That's funny.

LUKE sniffs.

LUKE: Mmmm. It's lovely. Mum's perfume!

HELEN: It's Repentance. You can wear it on your heart or on your pulse.

LUKE: Mum. You can come out now.

HELEN sniffs.

HELEN: Mum! I'm sorry we took so long. Your map wasn't very clear.

Silence. LUKE glances nervously towards the gate.

LUKE: Will pest come?

HELEN: (*Convincing herself.*) He was quite a nice cockroach. He said Repentance saves you from the meteorite. (*Startled.*) That man said it. (*Mimics.*) 'Repentance will save you.' We better pick some.

LUKE picks a rose. He pricks himself on a thorn.

He starts crying.

LUKE: Ow! I want to go home.

HELEN: It's only a thorn. Keep picking. I'm going to look for Mum.

LUKE resumes picking, putting the roses in the blanket.

LUKE: Blankit can carry them.

HELEN: (*As she climbs.*) It's really good you brought your blanket.

LUKE is very happy.

LUKE: Mum. Come back.
We've got repetals.
Mete-rite. Go away.
We've got repetals.

HELEN climbs the gatepost.

She sniffs. The smell of repentance is overwhelming.

HELEN: Mum. I'm sorry we took so long. It's my fault. I ate thirty-nine potato croquettes. (*Laughs.*) We got crumbs all over the map. Then I fell asleep. I think I missed the eleventh hour. But there'll be another one won't there?

HELEN's voice resonates and dies away.

Cockroach said a lady's here. It didn't sound like you. (*Laughs.*) He said she was a pest.

She looks down at the roses. She nearly falls off the gate.

(*Agitated.*) There's a lady. She's walking round those roses. Near where it said Anna. (*Uncertain.*) Mum? Her hair's all electric. Mum? It's Helen. Why don't you turn round? You can talk to me. (*Laughs.*) I won't tell Luke you're here, he'll only get in a tizzy. He's getting some Repentance to save us from the meteorite. (*Pause.*) I told him to. Stay there. Coming.

HELEN climbs down quickly.

The pink sky becomes fierier.

HELEN looks again but can't see the MOTHER.

She was there a minute ago.

HELEN realises she hasn't got the glasses on.

(*To LUKE. Angry.*) Where's Mum's glasses? Did you take them?

LUKE: No.

HELEN: I can't see properly without them. I can't read the map.

LUKE: Mete-rite did it.

HELEN: (*Nastily.*) Don't be a baby.

LUKE shows HELEN the contents of the blanket.

LUKE: (*Happily.*) Blankit's got repetals.

HELEN: (*Nastily.*) Repentance not repetals. Stop waving it around. Cockroach gets terrible hayfever.

HELEN steps by mistake ina puddle of water which is seeping under the gate.

(*Accussing.*) Now my feet are all wet.

HELEN's face goes funny as she tries not to cry.

LUKE: Sorry.

There is a crackle.

A light flashes, reflected in the puddle of tears.

HELEN and LUKE jump back.

Is it Mete-rite?

HELEN: The meteorite won't come here. We've got Repentance. Take it back to Andy. If Mete-rite comes you can make it go away. Don't drop it. Quick.

LUKE: (*Uncertainly.*) Mete-rite go away. We've got repetals.

LUKE hesitates.

HELEN: (*Impatient.*) Go on. Get lost.

LUKE: Where's Mum?

HELEN: (*Annoyed.*) She's not here. I'm going to find her glasses.

HELEN and LUKE set off in opposite directions.

LUKE picks up the blanket of flowers.

LUKE: Andy. Coming.

LUKE walks towards the gate.

HELEN sighs and tries one last time to read the map.

HELEN: It's all pink. (*She looks anxiously at the sky.*) Mum. Wait for me.

HELEN goes, wandering off through the garden.

Suddenly the pink sky becomes fierier as the shadow of the preacher looms up.

The PREACHER's voice echoes round the sky.

PREACHER'S VOICE: What are you doing in my garden?

LUKE: Blankit. You're coming with me.

LUKE runs towards the gate.

Scene 4

Outside the Garden of Repentance as in Scene Six.

LUKE crawls out under the gate dragging the blanket after him. He is terrified. He looks in the rubbish to see if the cockroach is there.

LUKE: (*Calling.*) Mr Cockroach. Where are you?

When he turns back, his path is barred by the PREACHER. The PREACHER is a very large man with a big shiny face dressed in a shiny silver suit. His black velvet shoes with gold buckles are too small for his feet. He wears a round necked shirt and a shiny gold necklace. His sandwich board reads: 'It's going to get worse' and the worse the news is, the happier he seems. His forearm is at right angles with his upper arm. His forefinger is permanently pointing. He moves his forearm up and down mechanically when he speaks, which he does in a strange voice, his words echo round the sky

PREACHER: Are you a *sinner*?
Or are you a *winner*?
You naughty boy.

LUKE: (*Calling.*) Helen. Come back. Mete-rite's here.

PREACHER: When a father says to his baby
DON'T DO THAT
What does the baby do? Eh?

LUKE: I'm not a baby.

PREACHER: (*Ignoring this.*) The baby does what he's told.
But you are naughty children.
A *meteorite* will come
And *blast* you to bits.

LUKE: (*Scared.*) Mr Cockroach. I want to go home.

LUKE is crying.

PREACHER: Only one thing will save you.

The PREACHER turns his back.

The word repentance is written on his sandwich board in silver letters.

What does it say?

LUKE: (*Panicky.*) Hat.

PREACHER: (*Louder.*) What does it say?

LUKE: HAT.

PREACHER: It says Repentance, you naughty boy.

The PREACHER turns round again. Miniature bottles are displayed along the ledge of his sandwich board.

(*Pleased.*) This is Repentance. You'd better ask your mother to buy you some.

LUKE: Our mum's away. She's been ages.

PREACHER: Then you must have been EXTREMELY naughty. You'll need a great deal

45

of Repentance. Do you have Repentance in your heart?

LUKE shows the blanket full of roses.

LUKE: (*Blurting out.*) I've got some here.

The PREACHER sees the roses in the blanket. He is very angry. There is a hissing, popping and crackling. The sky turns a fierier pink.

PREACHER: Stolen Repentance is no good at all. True Repentance has a bitter smell.

He throws a little bottle at LUKE.

It releases a horrible smell which makes LUKE cough and hold his nose.

LUKE: Ugh! It stinks like bad rubbish.

The PREACHER throws more bottles. They land on the rubbish pile. The COCKROACH's helmet and antennae roll out.

LUKE: Poor Mr Cockroach. You're naughty, Mete-rite. You killed cockroach with your stinky bottles.

LUKE breaks off a rose thorn. He pricks the PREACHER with it.

You're *extremely* naughty.

The PREACHER jumps into the air with shock.

The ground shakes as he lands.

PREACHER: Ow!

LUKE: It's only a thorn.

LUKE pricks the PREACHER again. He jumps into the air. As he lands he loses his balance and falls. The ground shakes.

You're going to squash our street. That's naughty.

PREACHER: (*Starting to sob.*) I never hurt a fly.

LUKE pricks the PREACHER again.

The PREACHER tries to defend himself.

PREACHER: Ow!

LUKE: (*Still pricking.*) You took our Mum's glasses and her letters.

PREACHER: (*Sobbing.*) That's an EXTREMELY naughty thing to say.

The PREACHER throws the rest of his bottles at LUKE.

PREACHER: Have some TRUE Repentance.

Again LUKE coughs and holds his nose.

LUKE: Stinky.

LUKE wafts his roses at the PREACHER. Some fall out and cover him.

LUKE: You have some TRUE repetals, Mete-rite.

The PREACHER is overcome with the smell. He lies on his back weeping. A puddle spreads out around him.

LUKE keeps wafting.

PREACHER: (*Weeping.*) I'm not a meteorite.

LUKE: Don't make things up. And stop crying. My feet are getting wet.

The PREACHER gets up, still weeping.

PREACHER: I wanted to save you with true repentance.

LUKE: Your repetals isn't true. Repetals is our Mum's perfume.

The PREACHER walks off slowly. His sorries echo round the sky.

LUKE keeps wafting the roses as he leaves.

PREACHER: (*Weeping as he goes.*) I'm very very very sorry. Very, very, very, very, very sorry. EXTREMELY sorry sorry sorry.

LUKE: (*After him.*) Get lost, Mete-rite. And don't come back.

LUKE goes off the way he and HELEN arrived, carrying the blanket.

END OF ACT TWO.

ACT THREE

Stopping the meteorite

Scene 1

*The street. The sky is ashen. The tree is stripped of branches
and reduced to a charcoal stump as if struck by lightning.
The spoons and forks have gone. LUKE enters with the
blanket of flowers.*

LUKE: (*Happily.*) No more mete-rite.

LUKE stops when he notices the tree.

LUKE: Oh no. Why have you stopped growing?
(*Sadly.*) No more potato crockits.

Pause.

LUKE: Mum! Are you ever coming back?

There is a crackling and a hissing.

Something shiny drops out of the sky.

LUKE examines the heavy object.

It's a parcel wrapped in foil.

Luke tries to pick it up.

LUKE: It's hot.

LUKE tears open the parcel.

LUKE: Mum's present. For when she comes home. Perfume. (*Pleased.*) True repetals. Mete-rite, why did you take our Mum's present? You took our letters and her glasses and the potato crockits. It's bad to take things.

He puts the perfume and wrapping in the blanket.

He wafts the roses around.

LUKE: Don't come back, Mete-rite.

LUKE wanders off still wafting the roses.

ANDY enters.

ANDY: Helen! Luke! I'm awake. I dreamed everything was burning. It's really hot. That's funny. There's a wind again. (*Sniffs.*) It smells different. Like flowers. It smells like Mum's perfume. Mum must be here. (*Excited.*) Mum!

ANDY sniffs the smell of roses.

ANDY: Mum! I didn't throw stones through Marino's Dad's window. (*Pause.*) I only wanted to see if it was strong. (*Pause.*) It was ages ago.

ANDY's voice resonates and dies away. Pause. ANDY takes out the mobile. He tries to dial. It plays a sad tune.

ANDY: Dad. You know when I asked about the meteorite? There's one coming and it's going to get everyone. You and all of us and Mum and Marino and Marino's Dad and all the other

people. How do you stop it? Dad? (*Pause.*) I'm
pressing the OK button.

*He presses the ok button. The distorted picture of the
mother appears and the message as before: 'Send your
picture. M.'*

ANDY: It's stuck. Never mind.

ANDY's face goes strange as he tries not to cry.

ANDY: (*Calls.*) Helen. I've got your mobile. (*Pause.*)
Luke. You're not really stupid.

ANDY's voice resonates and dies away.

*LUKE comes back with his blanket of roses. He's
wafting them around.*

LUKE: Don't come back Mete-rite. I've got Repetals.

ANDY: Luke. You've been ages. Mum must be
round here somewhere. There's this smell of
perfume. Where's Helen?

LUKE: She lost Mum's glasses. Look.

He shows ANDY the perfume.

LUKE: It's true Repetals. Mete-rite took it. Then it
fell down.

ANDY examines it.

ANDY: It's Mum's present. It's called Re-union.

LUKE: Repetals.

ANDY: (*Reads.*) Re-union stupid. It's a different
perfume.

LUKE: Oh.

LUKE shows ANDY the contents of the blanket.

LUKE: Look. I picked them in the garden with blankit. Then Mete-rite came. Then I made Mete-rite get lost.

ANDY is jealous.

ANDY: What did meteorite look like?

LUKE: Massive. Shiny. (*Pause.*) He had horrible stinky bottles.

ANDY: (*Sceptical.*) What did he say?

LUKE: (*Mimics.*) You're EXTREMELY naughty. Repetals will save you.

ANDY groans.

ANDY: Luke. That was the man. Remember?

LUKE: What man?

ANDY: We told you. The preacher. We saw him when we bought the presents.

LUKE: Not Mete-rite?

ANDY: Why've I got such a stupid brother? The meteorite's a rock. From outer space. It's getting nearer probably. The tree's all burnt.

LUKE takes his hat off. The sky turns very green. LUKE throws all the roses away.

LUKE: (*Sighs.*) Go away Repetals. You didn't stop Mete-rite.

ANDY: (*Sighs.*) I wish the sky would go normal.

ANDY leans against the gatepost in despair.

A bird shaped like a letter passes over. It sings a sad tune.

LUKE: (*Sighs.*) When Anna comes back will Mum come back?

ANDY: Luke. Anna's not coming back. We told you. (*Sighs.*) Mum won't come back probably. She's really cross.

Pause. LUKE tries to put his hat on top of ANDY's helmet. He giggles as it falls off.

LUKE: Mete-rite. Go away.

ANDY examines the hat.

ANDY: That's funny. It's made of foil.

ANDY takes off his helmet and puts the hat on properly.

The sky brightens.

He takes the foil hat out of his pocket and puts it on LUKE.

The sky brightens.

He takes the foil wrapping paper from the present and holds it up to the sky.

A corresponding clear patch appears in the sky.

ANDY: Look! The green's gone away.

ANDY jumps up.

ANDY: The foil did it. The green bounced off. If the meteorite comes...

He looks round the sky.

ANDY: It'll come from there probably. We'll hold up the foil like this and then it'll bounce off.

He holds up the foil wrapping paper.

Again, a bigger clear patch appears in the sky.

ANDY: Look at the sky. It's bright. The postman wasn't talking rubbish after all.

Scene 2

ANDY is still holding up the foil .The MOTHER appears in the bright patch of sky. Her face is strange. Her eyes are red. Her hair is electric. ANDY can't see her because the foil's in the way.

LUKE: Mumma!

LUKE runs towards her but, when she doesn't smile, he stops short.

Awkward pause.

ANDY is afraid to move the foil in case she disappears.

LUKE: (*To ANDY.*) Why is her face all funny?

There is a crackling and popping and hissing.

The MOTHER's voice is distorted and her words are scrambled. Only the word 'Anna' is distinguishable.

She doesn't look at the children.

MOTHER: Have you seen my baby?
I'm looking for Anna.
She had curly hair
And grey green eyes.

ANDY: (*Angry.*) She only knows one word. Anna.

ANDY kicks the roses that are lying on the ground. They land near the mother.

A lower level of crackling, popping and hissing.

MOTHER: (*More upset.*) I had a baby.
Her name was Anna.
She had curly hair.
I was asleep when she died.

ANDY is still holding up the foil though his arms are tired.

ANDY: (*Angry.*) Mum. Why don't you stop talking about Anna and talk to us instead?

Pause. The MOTHER looks at ANDY and LUKE.

LUKE: She's looking.

ANDY: Tell her I didn't throw stones.

LUKE: Mum. Why are your eyes all red? Are you cross?

Pause.

LUKE: Mum. Please come home. You've been ages.

The MOTHER starts to cry. Her eyes are no longer red.

The sky brightens.

LUKE: (*Happy.*) She's crying.

ANDY: (*Excited. To MOTHER.*) We've got a present. It's called Reunion. We unwrapped it for you.

LUKE: (*Excited.*) She wants to come home.

ANDY drops the foil.

The sky turns red.

The MOTHER disappears.

Scene 3

A crackle of thunder. The red light fills the sky. The postman's bag swings on the gatepost. The shadow of a strange bird shaped like a letter passes over. It sings a sad tune. The bird falls to the ground. The sky turns bright green. There is another crackle of thunder. Window frames rattle. There is a hissing, popping and crackling. Twigs and branches fall. The sky turns fiery pink.

Scene 4

ANDY and LUKE are smoothing the foil sheet which has been battered by the storm. It seems bigger than before.

HELEN enters. She is out of breath.

HELEN: (*Urgent.*) Andy. Luke. The meteorite's coming. I met the preacher. Near the train crossing. His suit was torn. He said all the repentance in the world is used up and there's nothing to stop the meteorite with. It'll be here any minute. (*Pause.*) What are you doing?

ANDY: It's foil. Like the postman said. The meteorite'll bounce off. We've got to hold it up. (*Points.*) It'll come from there probably.

LUKE: Can I hold it?

ANDY: Helen'll do it. (*To LUKE.*) You can wear your hat.

ANDY and HELEN hold up the foil sheet against the sky.

HELEN: I saw Mum. On the footbridge. After I went out of the garden. There was a different gate.

LUKE: Was she crying?

HELEN: No. She looked funny. She explained something.

ANDY: I know. It was about Anna.

HELEN: It's private. She said it didn't matter. About the glasses. Or the stones. Then I told her about

the meteorite and the repentance but she said we
didn't need any. Then she said go and find you
two.

LUKE: We saw her. She wants to come home.

*There is a loud crackling, hissing and popping. The
sky turns deep red.*

LUKE: Why's the sky full of fire?

ANDY: Hold it up.

*ANDY and HELEN stretch to hold up the sheet of
foil to the sky but with an even louder hiss, a
massive, shining fireball hurtles into the street from
an unexpected place. LUKE sees it first.*

LUKE: Mete-rite. Go away.

As the fireball lands he shouts.

LUKE: Mete-rite. Put your hat on.

*ANDY and HELEN capture and smother the
meteorite in the sheet of foil.*

*There is a hissing, popping and crackling as the sky
goes dark.*

Scene 5

The sky is ashen.

All that remains of the meteorite is a cold rock.

LUKE: Go away Mete-rite. And don't come back.

LUKE touches the rock.

HELEN: Careful. You'll burn yourself.

LUKE: It's cold.

ANDY: There's something falling.

LUKE: Letters!

HELEN: Ashes. From the sky. Where it was all burning.

ANDY: Water. It's rain.

The rain is silver. The children play in it. As they do this, the MOTHER appears in the same space as before. She's wearing a silver dress and crying silver tears. Her hair is no longer electric. Her eyes are no longer red. The phone falls out of ANDY's pocket. A light's flashing from it. It plays a happy tune.

LUKE: Bird's happy because Mete-rite's gone.

ANDY: It's a funny bird. It's the mobile.

He answers.

ANDY: Dad. (*To the others.*) Shh. (*He's listening.*) Nothing much. (*Pause. Lightly.*) Ok. (*To ANDY and LUKE.*) He's gone to pick up Mum from the station. He forgot to wake us up. He wants us to be ready with the presents.

HELEN, ANDY and LUKE: Yeah!

ANDY: (*To LUKE.*) Hold the phone. Hold it properly.

HELEN: Let's go together. I'm hiding my hair.

She puts some foil on her head.

ANDY and LUKE do likewise. They bunch together.

LUKE forgets the blanket.

ANDY takes the picture.

The three children's faces appear.

ANDY: One, two, three…

HELEN: Ok.

ANDY presses the OK button.

The sky goes dark.

ANDY: Everything's gone upside down again.

HELEN: No. It's the right way up.

The children tumble through the phone.

When the sky brightens the MOTHER's face appears.

She's not crying. It isn't strange.

Post Script

The street where the children live. The rock is still there. The gatepost is upright. The tree grows normally. HELEN enters. She is looking for somewhere to hide. She tries the tree but realises she can still be seen. She tries the gatepost but thinks better of it. As she hears ANDY, she runs to the rock and crouches behind it.

ANDY enters. He looks for HELEN behind the gatepost. He hides there for a second. He runs to the tree but HELEN isn't there. Then he notices the rock. He moves slowly towards it. As he climbs onto it, HELEN moves round the base of the rock out of sight. As ANDY jumps off the other side of the rock, HELEN breaks cover and runs to the gatepost.

HELEN hides behind the gatepost.

ANDY sees HELEN and scrambles over the rock to get her but by the time he gets to the gatepost she's back to the tree. By now they've seen each other and are out of breath and laughing.

HELEN sees an old perfume bottle on the ground. She picks it up.

HELEN: Look.

ANDY: What is it?

HELEN: Perfume. The label's gone. It's still full.

ANDY: It's that present. We were supposed to give to Mum. When she came back.

HELEN: We had to make another present really quick. (*Pause.*) We could give it to her now.

ANDY: Will she like it?

HELEN: Probably.

A door opens in one of the houses.

LUKE runs into the street.

LUKE: Helen! Andy! Mum says come now.

HELEN and ANDY hide.

LUKE: There's potato crockits.

LUKE climbs onto the rock.

LUKE: I can see you anyway.

LUKE jumps off the rock on the other side and runs back to the house. He disappears through the door.

HELEN breaks her cover first. She dashes from the tree to the rock, climbs onto it and jumps off the other side, closely followed by ANDY.

HELEN runs to the house. She goes through the door into the house and disappears.

ANDY follows through the door. He slams it behind him.

THE END.